TASTE THE WORLD!

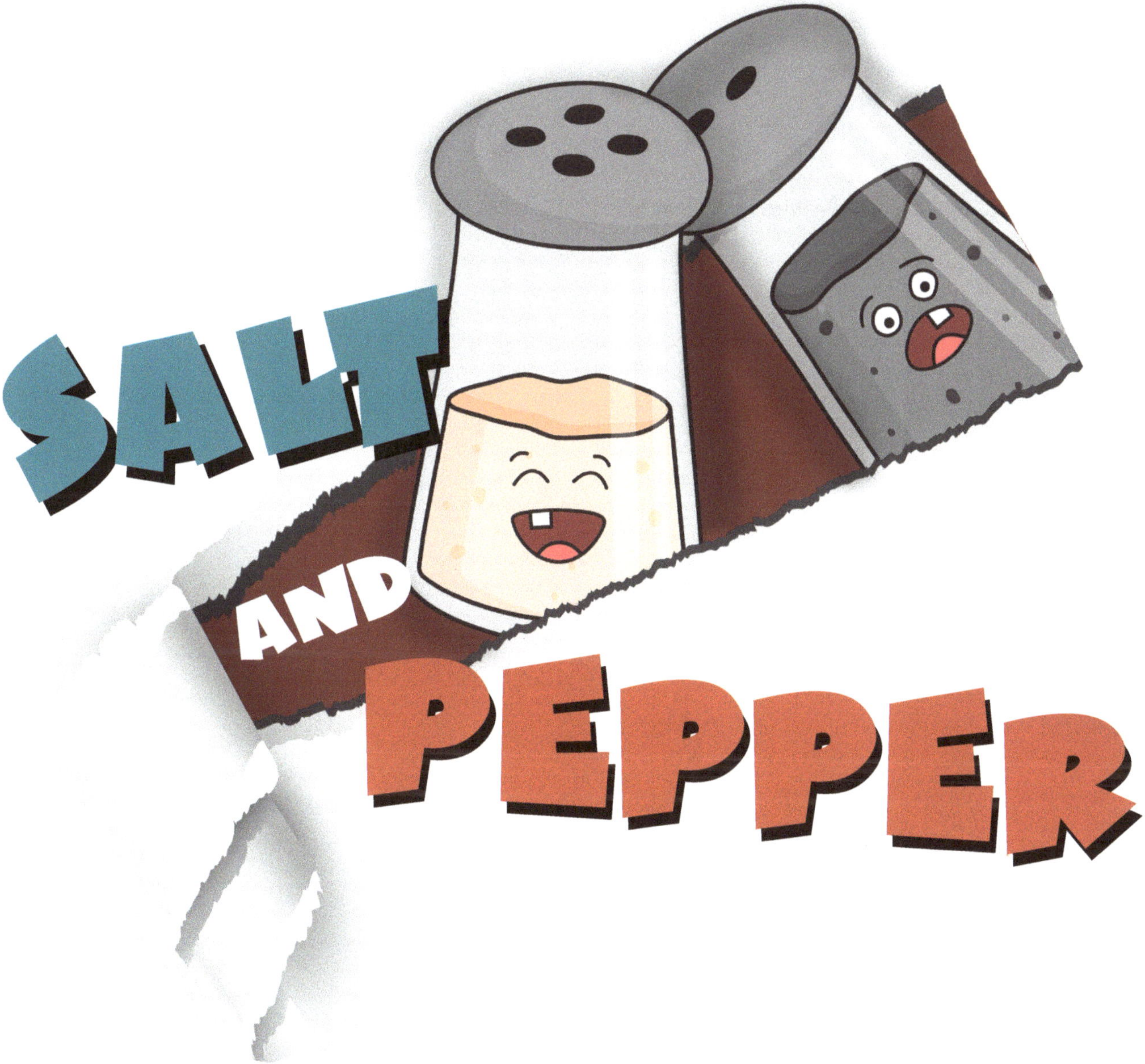

SALT AND PEPPER

www.worldbook.com

TABLE OF CONTENTS

4 I Am Salt! I Am Pepper!
6 What Is Salt?
8 A Look at Sea Salt and Rock Salt

10 CHINA

12 JAPAN
14 The Five Basic Tastes

16 MEDITERRANEAN
18 Types of Salt

20 SAHARA

22 INDIA

24 EUROPE

26 UNITED STATES

28 What Is Pepper?
30 A Look at the
     Pepper Plant

32 INDIA
34 Spice Routes

36 ITALY
38 CHINA
40 Age of Exploration
42 NEW WORLD
44 A Perfect Pair!
46 Glossary/Helpful Hints
47 Index
48 Acknowledgments

BEFORE YOU BEGIN

Included in this book are a few recipes that allow you to "taste the world!" Before you begin, look on page 46 for some helpful hints. Read the recipes carefully and always ask an adult to help—especially when handling knives or using the stove. Besides, cooking is easier and more fun when you work together!

ARE YOU HUNGRY FOR AN ADVENTURE IN FOOD? WE WILL BE YOUR TOUR GUIDES ON A TASTY JOURNEY AROUND THE WORLD TO LEARN ALL ABOUT US . . .
I AM SALT!

As we travel around the world, we'll explore our histories, discover some fun facts, and learn to prepare some delicious recipes. Along the way, you may read words that are new to you. If we can explain what a word means easily, we'll do it right where you are reading. If we use the word many times, or if the explanation is complicated, we will put the word in **boldface** (type that **looks like this**). Boldface words are defined in a glossary in the back of the book.

SALT?

Since ancient times, people have prized salt for its ability to give flavor to food. It has been called the "king of condiments"! This clear, brittle mineral is found naturally in the earth, in salt lakes, and in the ocean. Salt is highly valued by almost every culture in the world. It makes almost everything taste better!

Much of the table salt we buy today is *iodized*. That means it has a tiny amount of the element **iodine** added to it. People need just a bit of iodine in their diet for good health. Iodine is not found naturally in many foods. Adding iodine to table salt is an easy way to make sure people get the iodine they need.

SALTY TEARS!

Every cell in your body contains salt! An adult's body contains about 8.8 ounces (250 grams) of salt. No wonder your tears taste salty!

Salt used in food is made up of the chemical elements **sodium** and chlorine. Its chemical name is **sodium chloride. Table salt** is almost pure sodium chloride that has been ground into very tiny bits. Other kinds of salt have small amounts of various chemicals that give them slightly different characteristics.

NOT TOO MUCH NOR TOO LITTLE

It is not good for you to eat too much salt—but it can also be deadly if you do not get enough! Aim for 1,500 to 2,300 milligrams—less than a teaspoon—of salt a day from healthy foods.

Table salt looks white. But a closer look reveals it is actually made up of clear, almost perfect cubes!

A LOOK AT SEA SALT . . .

No matter where you find it, all salt comes from the seas! In some regions, people let seawater **evaporate** (dry up), then they collect the tiny pieces of **sea salt** that are left behind. Seawater is naturally salty. Evaporating seawater is one the oldest methods of producing salt.

SALTY SOURCE

The source of all the world's salt is **brine** (salty water) from oceans, seas, salt lakes, and other salty bodies of water. Even huge salt **deposits** (stores of minerals) deep underground were once part of the world's oceans. The deposits formed by the evaporation of seawater millions of years ago! If the salt in the ocean could be removed and spread evenly over Earth's land surface, it would form a layer more than 500 feet (150 meters) thick—about the height of a 40-story office building!

Much solar salt is produced in Australia, the Bahamas, China, India, Mexico, and near the Dead and Mediterranean seas. All of these places are warm and sunny. In the United States, solar salt is produced near Utah's Great Salt Lake.

. . . AND ROCK SALT

Salt that occurs in hard, massive layers beneath the ground is called **rock salt.** Underground salt deposits are found on every continent. People have been *mining* (digging) rock salt from underground deposits for thousands of years.

Some types of rock salt are used to melt ice.

The largest operating salt mine in the world is in Goderich in Ontario, Canada (above). The mine is under Lake Huron. It is 1,815 feet (553.21 meters) deep. Some of the largest underground salt deposits in the United States are the Salina Basin salts, in Michigan, Ohio, New York, Pennsylvania, and West Virginia.

DID YOU KNOW that some people visit salt mines because they believe they are healthful? The Salina Turda salt mine in Romania is a *halotherapy* (salt medicine) center and museum.

ONE OF THE FIRST PLACES TO PRODUCE SALT MAY HAVE BEEN

CHINA

Evidence of one of the earliest salt works dates to about 6000 B.C. in China. Salt was so important to the early Chinese that they even used coins made of salt as money! Today, China leads the world in salt production.

Although the Chinese are among the largest consumers of salt, they do not add salt to dishes at the table. But they do add salt to their many sauces!

THE WALL THAT SALT BUILT?

For over 2,600 years, China's government had complete control over the sale of salt. Taxes on salt may even have helped pay for the Great Wall of China!

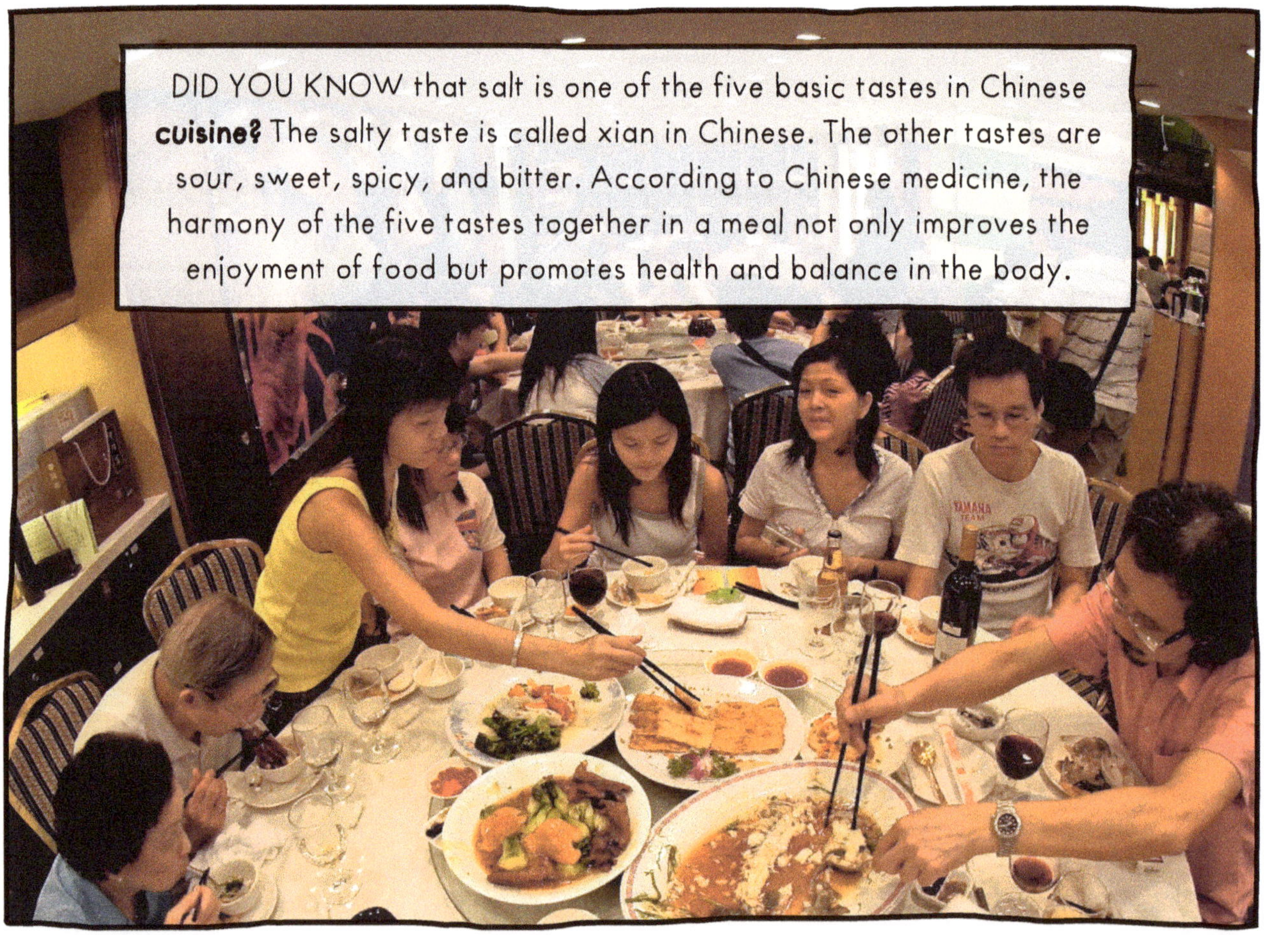

DID YOU KNOW that salt is one of the five basic tastes in Chinese **cuisine?** The salty taste is called xian in Chinese. The other tastes are sour, sweet, spicy, and bitter. According to Chinese medicine, the harmony of the five tastes together in a meal not only improves the enjoyment of food but promotes health and balance in the body.

Soy sauce is a salty, brown sauce made from **fermented** soybeans, roasted grain, brine, and special molds. Salt helps the fermentation process. Soy sauce originated in China centuries ago and has since become a central ingredient in many Asian cuisines. Many Chinese chefs add soy sauce to give food a salty and savory flavor.

SALT
S-T-R-E-T-C-H

Soy sauce may have been invented as a way to stretch out salt because it was so expensive.

Crescent-shaped dumplings called *jiaozi* are a traditional Chinese dish filled with meat or vegetables. They are served with a dipping sauce made of sesame oil, vinegar, minced garlic, chili paste, and soy sauce.

FOR THOUSANDS OF YEARS SALT HAS BEEN CONSIDERED SACRED IN 

Salt is one of the most important flavors that define Japanese cuisine. Together with two other ingredients from the sea—fish and seaweed—salt makes up the "holy trinity" that is the foundation of all Japanese cuisine.

Salt helps bring out the meaty **umami** (savory) flavor of foods—like salty **miso,** made from fermented soybeans—that the Japanese people savor. Salt is used to prepare dried fish and **pickled** vegetables—ingredients that are used in almost every dish.

SALT RELEASES MOISTURE!

Adding salt to raw ingredients will draw out moisture. Salting such juicy vegetables as cucumbers helps remove moisture so that dressings will not become watery when added to a cucumber dish. Salt also reduces the bitter taste of some foods.

Sunomono is a Japanese cucumber salad served with a meal. It is made with a sweet and tangy marinade of vinegar, sugar, and soy sauce and sprinkled with sesame seeds.

Japan has five seas. Salts from these seas each have their own special taste, depending on the climate, geography, mineral content, marine life, and *salinity* (salt concentration). Tastes range from spicy and herblike to sour, mellow, or sweet.

In Shinto, the traditional religion of Japan, salt is associated with purification. At mealtime, the Japanese place a small cup or dish of salt on the table. This is meant as a purification ritual. But diners may also use salt from the dish to flavor their food.

GET IN THE RING

Sumo wrestlers scatter salt to symbolically cleanse and purify the ring. This ritual is more than 1,500 years old.

DID YOU KNOW that in Japan, salt is sprinkled on ice cream? A tiny amount of salt enhances the sweetness and improves the flavor balance. There is even ice cream made with soy sauce!

THE FIVE BASIC TASTES

How would you describe something you just ate—would it be sweet, sour, salty, or bitter? Our taste buds help us identify what the taste is. Taste buds are little bumps on your tongue.

In addition to these four tastes, some scientists think there is a fifth taste that is "savory" or "meaty." This taste is called *umami.*

Japanese scientists were the first to describe umami. The sensation of umami is caused by a saltlike chemical called **glutamate.** Glutamate is found in many protein-rich foods. It also enhances the flavor of foods.

PASS THE UMAMI, PLEASE!

Salt brings out the umami flavor in food.

Mushrooms and Parmesan cheese have a rich umami taste.

TRY THIS!

This dip features the umami flavor of miso. It is best served chilled with your favorite veggies!

SAVORY RANCH DIP

Makes 1 ½ cups

INGREDIENTS

4 oz. drained soft (silken) tofu
2 tbsp. white miso
1 tbsp. fresh lemon juice
2 tsp. sherry vinegar or white wine vinegar
½ tsp. garlic powder
½ tsp. onion powder
¼ tsp. freshly ground black pepper

½ cup sour cream
1 tbsp. chopped fresh flat-leaf parsley
2 tbsp. finely chopped fresh chives plus more for garnish
Fresh raw vegetables, cut up into bite-sized pieces

STEPS

1. In a blender, mix lemon juice, miso, garlic powder, onion powder, pepper, tofu, and vinegar on high speed.
2. Stir in sour cream, parsley, and 2 tablespoons of chives. Place dip in a small serving bowl and chill in the refrigerator.
3. When ready to serve, garnish with additional chopped chives, if desired. Serve with raw vegetables for dipping.

DID YOU KNOW that *umami* is the Japanese word for *deliciousness?*

MEDITERRANEAN

In ancient times, the Mediterranean Sea was at the crossroads of trade routes that spread between Italy, Spain, Greece, and Egypt. Such cities as Genoa, Pisa, and Venice in Italy developed as major centers for the salt trade. Salt was so valuable in this region that lumps of salt called salt cakes could be used as money!

The Mediterranean region is famous for its olives. Fresh olives taste bitter and are unpleasant to eat. To make olives taste good, they are soaked in brine or a salty solution called **lye** to remove the bitterness.

OLIVE YOU, SALT!

As olives ripen, they turn from green to yellow to red to purple-black. The olives people eat are either green or black. Then they are washed and fermented in brine.

DID YOU KNOW that people in ancient Mesopotamia, in the eastern Mediterranean region, pickled food? *Pickling* means to preserve foods in brine, vinegar, or other liquid. Pickling is one of the oldest methods of food preservation.

Koshari is an Egyptian dish that has been made since the 1800's. It mixes together rice, macaroni, lentils, and chickpeas, and is topped off with a spicy tomato sauce and fried onions. Brining and salting help beans and peas cook more quickly and evenly. Salt works to soften the skin of beans and peas and allows the water to soak in. The salty water also adds to the wonderful flavor.

The Italian island of Sicily was a Mediterranean trading hub for salt. A classic Sicilian dish is fish baked in salt. The fish is "buried" in the salt, like sand. As it bakes, the salt sets to a crust, holding the moisture in the fish. When the fish is done, the crust is cracked open. It peels off in large chunks, revealing the moist, delicious fish inside.

NATRON

Natron is a type of salt that was used by ancient Egyptians to preserve mummies. It is still found in Egypt today.

A LOOK AT SOME COMMON
TYPES OF SALT

All salt is made up mainly of sodium chloride. Yet a small amount of *impurities* (other substances) can give ordinary salt remarkable qualities. Professional chefs know that using the right kind of salt in a particular dish can make all the difference in the world! There are thousands of varieties of salt in the world. Here are a few of the more common kinds.

TABLE SALT

This is the salt in most salt shakers. It is almost pure sodium chloride crystals. Table salt is white and made up of fine grains that appear as perfect tiny cubes. Just as the name says, this salt is most commonly found on tables, where diners can add it to their food as they like.

FLEUR DE SEL

In French, this means *flower of salt*. This salt is gathered by hand with wooden rakes from the ocean shore in Brittany, in northern France. As a natural sea salt, it has many other minerals that give it a bluish color and rich taste. It is one of the most expensive kinds of salt. It is used to add a dash of flavor to meat, fish, vegetables, and even chocolate!

HIMALAYAN SALT

This salt is harvested by hand from the Khewra Salt Mine in the Himalaya of Pakistan. This salt varies in color from white to bright pink. It is rich in minerals. Some people consider it the healthiest kind of salt. Its mineral content gives it a bold flavor. The salt retains heat well and large blocks of this salt are even used as serving platters!

SNIFF!

Salt helps release *aroma* (scent) molecules from food into the air. Your sense of smell works together with your taste buds to define flavors.

KOSHER SALT

Kosher is a Hebrew word that means *fit* or *proper*. Kosher food is food prepared according to the strict ancient Jewish dietary laws. Kosher salt has large, irregular grains. It is easily sprinkled on foods and it dissolves quickly, making it a perfect all-purpose cooking salt.

SEA SALT

This salt is obtained by evaporating seawater. It has naturally occurring minerals that give it a hint of other flavors. It is ideal for people who wish to limit the amount of salt in their diet.

SAHARA

The great empires of West Africa, Ghana, Mali, and Songhai thrived from about 300 A.D. to the late 1500's. These magnificent empires were rich in gold, but poor in salt. They had to trade for it. The people who lived around the Sahara of North Africa, the world's largest desert, could easily mine salt. They carried salt across the Sahara on long camel caravans. One camel caravan in the 1300's was said to have had more than 12,000 camels! That's a lot of salt!

Camel caravans carried large slabs of salt across the Sahara to such cities as Djenne and Timbuktu on the Niger River. There, salt was traded for gold—as well as ivory, skins, kola nuts, pepper, and sugar.

DID YOU KNOW that bread is considered sacred in Morocco? Every meal includes bread. A little salt in bread dough will contribute to a golden crust. Salt also helps the yeast to develop and form a fine texture.

DON'T SPILL THE SALT!

Spilling salt is considered bad luck. In the past, salt was so expensive, it was thought that wasting it would be like throwing your money away. To reverse the luck, toss a little salt over your left shoulder!

Kyinkyinga is a type of beef **kabob** that is a popular street food in Ghana, Nigeria (where a slightly different version called *suya kebab* is served), and other West African countries. It is made with a rub of ground peanuts, spices, and salt and pepper.

SALTING MAKES MEAT JUICY!

Seasoning meats with salt or a salty spice rub helps meat hold on to its own natural juices. When salt is applied to raw meat, protein-rich juices inside the meat are drawn to the surface. The salt then dissolves in the released liquid. It forms a brine that is reabsorbed by the meat. During cooking, the juice dries on the meat's surface, creating a crisp, delicious crust.

In 326 B.C., the Macedonian general Alexander the Great is believed to have visited the Khewra Salt Mine in what is now Pakistan. Today, this salt mine still produces the famous pink Himalayan salt that is enjoyed all over the world!

Farsan are salty snacks served with tea in Gujarat, a state in northwestern India. Farsan may be deep-fried, then dried and stored. They can be fresh or steamed, spicy or simple. *Khandvi* is a healthy, savory type of farsan. This yellowish snack is made with *gram* (chickpea) flour, yogurt, ginger paste, water, salt, turmeric, and chili pepper rolled tightly into bite-sized pieces. Khandvi is usually served with garlic chutney for a wonderful blend of taste sensations!

Kala namak, or Himalayan black salt, is a famous type of Indian volcanic salt. It is heated, then mixed with Indian spices and herbs. Black salt has a savory taste. It is used along with other spices in many Indian dishes including **chutneys,** pickles, salads, and *raitas* (yogurtlike condiments).

SALT MARCH FOR FREEDOM

In 1930, the Indian leader Mohandas K. Gandhi led 78 followers 240 miles (386 kilometers) to the sea to make salt from seawater. At that time, India was under British rule and people had to buy salt from the British government. It was a crime to get salt anywhere else. Gandhi's acts of nonviolent protest helped India become a free nation.

Europeans value salt not only for enhancing the taste of their favorite foods, but also for preserving fish.

The coast of the North Sea in northern Europe is an especially important source of fish. Countries along the coast have their own special ways of enjoying salted fish. A Dutch tradition is herring prepared in brine and spices. It is served with raw onions and *gherkins* (small pickled cucumbers) on a bun. Or, throw your head back and eat it the Dutch way!

Salt is used in most cheese recipes. The kind used is often called cheese salt. It is non-iodized salt. Iodized salt keeps bacteria from growing. Cheese needs bacteria for ripening. This gives cheese its flavor and texture. Salt also controls moisture and causes the *curds* (solid lumps) to shrink. This helps form a good rind. Salt also adds to the flavor of the cheese.

Germany is famous for its pretzels! This twisted biscuit has a delicious glazed, salted surface. The first pretzels were made in the early 600's by European monks for children. THIS RECIPE REQUIRES ADULT SUPERVISION.

TRY THIS!

SALTY SOFT PRETZELS

Makes 8 pretzels

INGREDIENTS

1 ½ cups warm water
1 tbsp. sugar
1 envelope active dry yeast
2 tsp. kosher salt
4 ½ cups all-purpose flour
2 oz. unsalted butter, melted

vegetable oil
10 cups water
⅔ cup baking soda
1 large egg yolk beaten with 1 tbsp. water
pretzel salt or coarse sea salt

STEPS

1. In the bowl of a stand mixer, combine warm water, sugar, and kosher salt. Dissolve the yeast in this liquid mixture and let it rest for 5 minutes. (A foam will begin to form on top.) Using the dough hook attachment, mix in the flour and butter on a low speed until well combined. Increase the speed to medium and knead until the dough pulls away from the sides of the bowl, about 4 to 5 minutes. Transfer the dough to a large bowl that has been coated with oil. Roll the dough in the bowl into a round shape so that it gets a light coating of oil. Cover it with plastic wrap and a dish towel. Let it rest in a warm place for 50 to 55 minutes, or until the dough has doubled in size.
2. Preheat the oven to 450 °F (232 °C). Line two baking sheets with parchment paper. Lightly brush with vegetable oil. Set aside.
3. HAVE AN ADULT bring the 10 cups of water and the baking soda to a boil in a large pot.
4. While waiting for the water to boil, place the dough on a lightly floured work surface and divide it into 8 equal parts. Roll one part into a snake shape about 2 feet long. Bring the two ends toward you, twist one over the other and criss-cross them. Dipping your finger in little bit of water, dampen the ends and lightly press them onto the dough snake as shown in the photo. Carefully place the pretzel on the parchment-lined cookie sheet. Repeat with the remaining sections.
5. HAVE AN ADULT carefully lower one pretzel into the boiling water with a slotted skimmer. Let it stay in the water for 30 seconds and then transfer it back to the parchment-lined baking sheet. Repeat this step for each pretzel.
6. Brush the top of each pretzel with the egg yolk and water mixture and then sprinkle with pretzel salt or coarse sea salt.
7. Bake until dark golden brown, about 12 to 14 minutes. Let them cool on a rack for 10 minutes. Enjoy the pretzels warm!

UNITED STATES

After the American Revolution, saltworks were set up along the Atlantic Coast for boiling seawater. A salt industry also grew up near Syracuse, New York, where salt springs were discovered. The Erie Canal, completed in 1825, was built to transport salt and other goods from Syracuse to other cities. The canal became known as "the ditch that salt built."

Before refrigeration was invented, salt was used to preserve meat. This process is called **curing.** Curing food remains popular because people enjoy the flavor created from the process. Special kinds of salts are usually used to cure food. Ham and bacon— as well as all-American hot dogs—are modern examples of cured meats.

DID YOU KNOW that Americans eat 20 billion hot dogs a year? That's about 70 hot dogs per person each year!

Cucumbers preserved in brine are called *pickles* in the United States. Americans didn't invent pickles. But pickles are an important part of American culture. By 1659, Dutch farmers began growing cucumbers around New York City. Dealers bought the cucumbers, pickled them in brine, and sold them out of barrels on the street. In the late 1800's and early 1900's, Eastern European Jews arrived and introduced kosher dill pickles to America. What better way to enjoy a hot dog!

TRY THIS!

Here's an easy pickle recipe worth preserving! Keep these pickles in the refrigerator.

CRUNCHY DILL PICKLES

Makes 2 quarts

INGREDIENTS

- 10-12 pickling cucumbers, cut into ¼-inch slices or spears
- 4 cups water
- 2 cups white vinegar
- 2 tbsp. kosher salt
- 1 tsp. sugar
- 15-20 stems fresh dill
- 8-12 cloves peeled garlic
- 8-10 peppercorn kernels

STEPS

1. For the brine, place water, vinegar, salt, and sugar in medium sauce pan. HAVE AN ADULT bring the solution to a boil. Lift the pan and swirl the salt and sugar to help it dissolve. Remove from heat and cool to room temperature.
2. Place some of the dill, garlic, and peppercorns in the bottom of two clean, sterile one-quart canning jars. Place about half of the cucumbers in the jar, leaving some room for the brine.
3. Add more dill, garlic, and peppercorns to the jars. Pour in enough brine to cover the cucumbers. Seal with an airtight lid. Store in the refrigerator for at least one week before eating. Pickles should be good for another 4 to 6 weeks.

IN A PICKLE

The word *pickle* comes from the Dutch *pekel* or northern German *pókel*, meaning *salt* or *brine*.

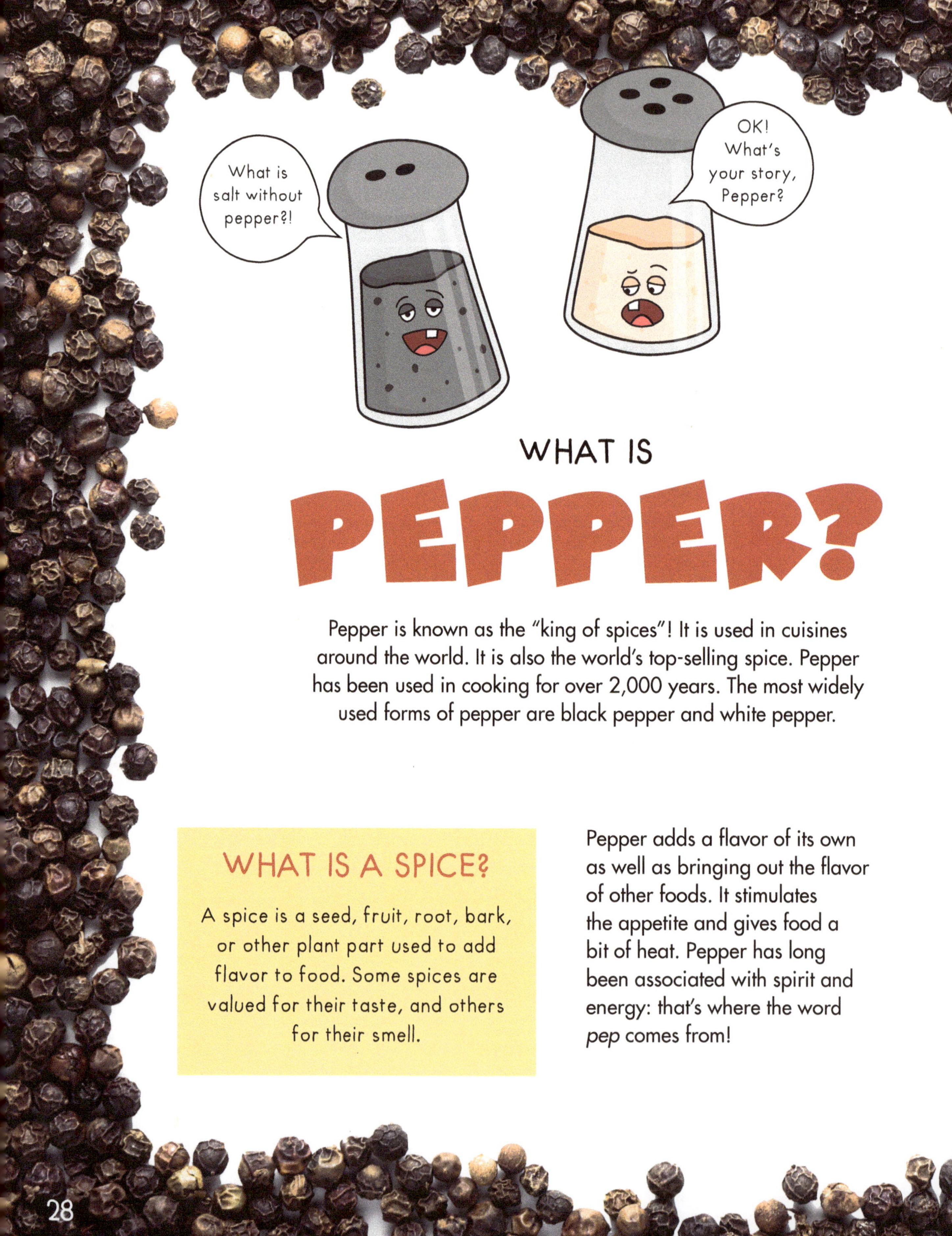

WHAT IS
PEPPER?

Pepper is known as the "king of spices"! It is used in cuisines around the world. It is also the world's top-selling spice. Pepper has been used in cooking for over 2,000 years. The most widely used forms of pepper are black pepper and white pepper.

WHAT IS A SPICE?

A spice is a seed, fruit, root, bark, or other plant part used to add flavor to food. Some spices are valued for their taste, and others for their smell.

Pepper adds a flavor of its own as well as bringing out the flavor of other foods. It stimulates the appetite and gives food a bit of heat. Pepper has long been associated with spirit and energy: that's where the word *pep* comes from!

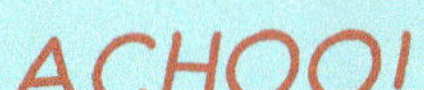

ACHOO!

Peppercorns were found stuffed into the nostrils of the pharaoh Ramses II, a famous mummy from ancient Egypt. The Egyptians believed pepper cleansed the body.

Pepper is sold ground or as **peppercorns** (dried berries). Peppercorns are crushed or ground up with a pepper grinder.

DID YOU KNOW that ground pepper quickly loses its flavor and aroma? The outer shell of the whole peppercorn seals in the flavor but once it is ground, it loses flavor and aroma within 30 days.

Like salt, pepper was once a precious item that only the rich could afford. But today we see pepper alongside salt on dining tables all over the world! How did these two become a pair? Read on to find out!

But first let's learn a bit about where pepper comes from...

A LOOK AT THE PEPPER PLANT...

The pepper plant is a spreading vine that grows today in the hot climates of Brazil, India, Indonesia, and Vietnam.

The plant produces small green berries that turn red as they ripen. The berries are harvested when they just begin to change color. They are cleaned and dried. As they dry, the berries turn black. The dried berries are often called peppercorns. Black pepper is the kind used in most homes.

BLACK PEPPERCORN

COLORFUL PEPPERCORNS

Black, green, white, and red peppercorns are all the same fruit!

WHITE PEPPERCORN

Fresh green pepper is used in some Asian cuisines, including dishes in Thailand. Green pepper has a fresh and spicy taste and bright aroma. It spoils quickly, so it is often dried or pickled.

GREEN PEPPERCORN

White pepper is made from fully ripe berries. The berries are washed and dried, then the skin is removed. White pepper has a finer flavor than black pepper and is not as strong.

RED PEPPERCORN

Red peppercorns are hot and spicy and a bit fruity tasting. The berries are left on the vine until they turn bright red. Red peppercorns are often found in pepper mixes. The berries spoil quickly, so they are often brined, freeze-dried, or air-dried.

Why does pepper make us sneeze? A substance called *piperine* may irritate the nostrils and cause people to sneeze. No one knows for sure!

PEPPERS OF A DIFFERENT KIND

Other spices are sometimes called pepper but are made from different plants. For example, a spice called *red pepper,* or *cayenne pepper,* is not true pepper and is made from an unrelated plant. Allspice, sometimes called *Jamaica pepper* or *pimento,* is not true pepper either.

INDIA

Unlike salt, which can be found or made just about everywhere in the world, pepper originally grew in only one place—India. It still grows today in the lush rain forests in the southwest province of Kerala. Kerala became famous in the ancient world for its pepper.

By 2000 B.C., pepper was widely used in Indian cooking. Today, India is one of the largest producers of pepper and its largest consumer.

THE WORLD'S FINEST PEPPER

Tellicherry black peppercorns, named for a city in Kerala, are considered the finest in the world. These extra-large berries are left on the vine longer than most pepper, so they develop a deep, rich flavor.

Garam masala is a spice blend used in Indian cuisine that features pepper alongside ground spices. Its name means *hot spices* in Hindi, one of the official languages of India.

This all-purpose seasoning adds warm, sweet flavor to chicken, fish, lamb, potatoes, rice, and breads.
For a quick and easy version, mix together in a bowl: 1 tablespoon ground cumin, 1 ½ teaspoons ground coriander, 1 ½ teaspoons ground cardamom, 1 ½ teaspoons ground black pepper, 1 teaspoon ground cinnamon, ½ teaspoon ground cloves, and ½ teaspoon ground nutmeg. Place mix in an airtight container, and store in a cool, dry place.

SPICE ROUTES

Traders from as far away as Europe brought gold to India and took away pepper. Historians believe Alexander the Great introduced pepper to Greece from India around 320 B.C. Pepper became a major ingredient in ancient Greek and Roman cooking between 100 and 300 A.D. From there, the popularity of pepper spread across Europe.

BLACK GOLD

Peppercorns were known as "black gold" because of their value. In ancient Greece, pepper was used like money. The Romans sometimes demanded pepper as a ransom when attacking a city. In the Middle Ages, a man's wealth was measured by his stockpile of pepper!

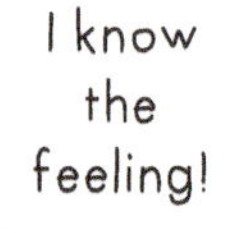

DID YOU KNOW that the ancient Greek physician Hippocrates used pepper as a medicine?

TRY THIS!

Pepper in a dessert? Why not? Many countries have their own versions of black pepper cookies. This version adds chocolate to the batter to make it even more delicious. The black pepper brings out the chocolate flavor and gives the cookie a little bit of zing!

BLACK PEPPER CHOCOLATE COOKIES

Makes 18-24 cookies

INGREDIENTS

- ½ tsp. vanilla
- ¾ cup flour
- ¼ cup unsweetened cocoa powder
- 1 tsp. baking powder
- ½ tsp. finely ground black pepper
- 4 tbsp. salted butter, softened
- 6 tbsp. sugar plus extra for flattening dough
- 4 tbsp. brown sugar
- 1 egg
- 4 oz. semisweet chocolate chips

STEPS

1. Sift the flour, cocoa powder, baking powder, and pepper in a bowl. Set aside.
2. Using a mixer, blend the butter and sugars until creamy. Beat in the egg and vanilla until they are well incorporated.
3. Add the dry, sifted ingredients until just blended. Do not overmix.
4. Stir in the chocolate chips by hand.
5. Cover the bowl with plastic wrap and chill in the refrigerator for at least an hour.
6. Line a baking sheet with parchment paper. Drop the batter by the teaspoonful onto the baking sheet, about 1 inch apart. Using the bottom of a glass dipped in sugar, flatten the dough slightly. Bake in a preheated oven at 350 °F (175 °C) for 10 to 12 minutes, until firm to the touch. Transfer the cookies to a wire rack to cool.

ROMAN RECIPES

The ancient Roman cookbook, *Apicius,* uses black pepper in almost all of its recipes. It even recommended using pepper in sweet desserts!

ITALY

Pepper is a beloved spice in Italy today. Italian cuisine uses black pepper in more kinds of dishes than just about any other cuisine!

Italian meals are gatherings of family and friends. Black pepper makes its first appearance in an Italian meal with the **antipasto** (appetizers) tray. This course is served before the pasta. The antipasto may consist of a variety of cold meats, including *prosciutto* (spiced ham), salami, mortadella, guanciale, and speck alto adige; such vegetables as olives and artichoke hearts; and such cheeses as *pecorino pepato* (raw sheep's milk cheese dotted with black peppercorns).

TUTTO SALE E PEPE!

In Italian, if you are *tutto sale e pepe (all salt and pepper),* it means you are happy and fun to be around!

A famous peppery Italian dish is *pasta alla carbonara.* It is made with egg, hard cheese (such as Parmesan or Romano), guanciale or pancetta (Italian bacon), such pasta as spaghetti, and of course, lots of pepper! This spice adds heat and a roasted flavor to the basic pasta.

One of the most well-known Italian dishes that uses pepper is *cacio e pepe*. It is made with three basic ingredients: cheese, pasta, and cracked black pepper. Together, these ingredients create a delicious and nourishing blend of flavors to satisfy your hunger!

SPAGHETTI CACIO E PEPE

Serves 2-3

(SPAGHETTI WITH CHEESE AND BLACK PEPPER)

INGREDIENTS

kosher salt
8 oz. spaghetti
3 tbsp. unsalted butter, cubed, divided

1 tsp. freshly cracked black pepper
1 cup finely grated Parmesan cheese
⅓ cup finely grated Pecorino cheese

STEPS

1. HAVE AN ADULT bring 3 quarts of water to a boil in a 5-quart pot. Season with salt. Add pasta, and following box directions, cook until almost *al dente* (firm to the tooth). Stir occasionally. Drain the pasta, saving ¾ cup of the cooking water.
2. Meanwhile, melt 2 tablespoons of the butter in a heavy skillet over medium heat. Add the pepper, and swirling the pan, cook until toasted, about one minute.
3. Add ½ cup of the reserved cooking water to the skillet and bring to a simmer. Add the drained pasta and remaining butter. Reduce heat to low and add the Parmesan cheese. Toss with tongs until melted. Remove pan from heat. Add the Pecorino cheese. Toss until cheese melts and the sauce coats the pasta.
If the sauce seems dry, add more pasta water.
Serve in warm bowls.

DID YOU KNOW that this dish was originally prepared by shepherds in Italy? The ingredients were affordable and nourishing. Cheese provides protein. **Carbohydrates** in the pasta provide energy. Pepper generates body heat, which helped keep the shepherds warm during the cold winter.

CHINA

Pepper reached China a bit later than other regions. It was first mentioned in Chinese writings around 200 A.D., but was not well known then. By the 1100's, black pepper had become a popular ingredient in the cuisine of China's wealthy and powerful.

STRANGER IN TOWN

When pepper came to China, it was referred to in texts as *hujiao* (barbaric or foreign pepper).

Marco Polo wrote that during his journey to China in the 1200's, he heard that the city of Kinsay (now Hangzhou) imported 10,000 pounds (4,500 kilograms) of pepper a day!

In the 1400's, the Chinese navigator Zheng He and his fleet brought back a large amount of peppercorns from his voyages beyond the South China Sea and Indian Ocean. Pepper went from a precious luxury to a common spice in China.

SZECHUAN (NOT A) PEPPER

Szechuan pepper is a popular spice from south-central China. Despite its name, it is not closely related to either black pepper or the chili pepper. It has a lemony taste and a different kind of spicy heat that creates a tingly numbness in the mouth.

Today, pepper has become an important ingredient in Chinese food. The Chinese prefer white pepper, made from the ripe fruit seeds. White pepper is fruitier, with an earthy or smoky flavor. It is used to add extra flavor to Chinese soups, stir fries, and marinades for meat.

AGE OF EXPLORATION

Pepper was important in the global spice trade. The demand for pepper and other spices led Christopher Columbus to seek a sea route to Asia, a voyage on which he became the first European to visit the New World.

The Portuguese explorer Vasco da Gama also sought pepper. He set out to find a faster route to India for spice-hungry Europeans. His ships rounded the southern tip of Africa and entered the Indian Ocean. In 1498, da Gama reached India. His voyage led the way for ocean trade between Europe and Asia. Portugal soon became a leading power in the spice trade.

By the 1500's, pepper had become an important export crop in Dutch-controlled Sumatra, an island in western Indonesia. At the time, Portugal controlled most of the spice trade in the region. In the 1600's, the Netherlands, along with England, Denmark, and France formed the East India Company. They seized Portuguese holdings and drove the Portuguese traders out of India. Later, as the British Empire grew in power, the British East India Company took control of the spice trade.

NEW WORLD

In the 1600's, the Portuguese introduced pepper to what is now Brazil, in South America. Pepper thrived in the hot climate. In 1933, Japanese immigrants from Singapore started growing pepper on a major scale in Brazil. Today, Brazil is one of the most important producers and exporters of pepper.

Other places in Latin America where pepper is grown include Mexico, Guatemala, Honduras, Saint Lucia, Costa Rica, and Puerto Rico. In all these places, pepper was grown from vines taken from Brazil.

DID YOU KNOW? Although Brazil is a major grower of pepper, most Brazilians do not much like black pepper or spicy foods!

When pepper arrived in the Americas, regional cuisines began incorporating it into their foods with native spices and herbs to create unique spice blends. In the Caribbean, a seasoning blend called Jamaican jerk was invented. It features black pepper, chilies, thyme, cinnamon, garlic, and nutmeg. It is sprinkled on vegetables or meats.

Cajun seasoning is a spicy blend featuring lots of black pepper, paprika, cayenne, garlic powder, and oregano. *Cajuns* are a people in southern Louisiana and eastern Texas who trace their ancestry to French settlers called *Acadians.* Cajun seasoning can be sprinkled on everything from chicken to seafood, vegetables to potatoes, soups to stir fries, and dips.

HEALTHY AND DELICIOUS!

Black pepper on food helps the body absorb more valuable vitamins and nutrients from the food more easily.

A crust made out of crushed peppercorns is a unique way of adding subtle flavor to a roast. A trick to reduce the heat of the pepper is to simmer the peppercorns in a pan with some olive oil for a few minutes, then place them on a paper towel to drain. Preparing the roast with a rub of salt, sugar, and baking soda will create a surface like a magnet, helping the peppercorns to stick when they are pressed into the meat.

A PERFECT PAIR!

Until the 1600's, pepper was usually added in the kitchen. Salt was presented on the table in a fancy silver vessel called a *saltcellar*. It was usually served with a spoon because it often attracted moisture and became lumpy. By the 1700's, pepper shakers began to join saltcellars on the dining table.

Salt shakers became common in the early 1900's, when salt producers figured out how to keep table salt from clumping. Salt and pepper shakers have been a pair ever since!

DID YOU KNOW that at first, the salt shaker usually had only one hole and the pepper shaker had two or three?

Salt and pepper shakers became collectible items after the development of the automobile. People could travel about freely while on vacation. The shakers were cheap, colorful, and easy to carry. They made great souvenirs and gifts.

MUSEUM PIECES

A fan of salt and pepper shakers has collected over 40,000 pairs—enough to fill two museums! Half of the collection is at the Museum of Salt and Pepper Shakers in Gatlinburg, Tennessee; the other half is in Guadalest, Spain.

GLOSSARY

antipasto *(AHN tee PAHS toh)* An appetizer or assortment of appetizers consisting of fish, meats, deviled eggs, peppers, lettuce, olives, and other vegetables.

brine *(bryn)* Very salty water.

carbohydrate *(KAHR boh HY drayt)* Carbohydrates are made up of carbon, hydrogen, and oxygen. Sugar and starch are carbohydrates.

chutney *(CHUHT nee)* A spicy sauce or relish made of fruits, herbs, pepper, and other seasoning.

cuisine *(kwih ZEEN)* A style of cooking or preparing food.

cure *(kyur)* To preserve meat, fish, or other food, especially by drying, salting, smoking, or pickling.

deposit *(dih POZ iht)* A mass of some mineral in rock or in the ground.

evaporation *(ih VAP uh RAY shuhn)* When a liquid or a solid changes into a gas.

ferment *(fuhr MEHNT)* A biological process carried out by microbes, such as bacteria, molds, and yeasts, that breaks down materials.

glutamate *(GLOO tuh mayt)* A salt or compound of glutamic acid.

iodine *(Y uh dyn)* A chemical element. Plants and animals need traces of iodine for normal growth.

kabob *(kuh BOB)* Roasted meat.

lye *(ly)* A strong solution that neutralizes acids and forms salts with them.

miso *(MEE soh)* A Japanese vegetable paste made from fermented soybean curds.

natron *(NAY tron)* A powdery mineral consisting of sodium carbonate and salt.

peppercorn *(PEHP uhr KAWRN)* One of the dried berries or fruits that are ground up to make pepper.

pickle *(PIHK uhl)* To preserve in salt water (brine).

piperine *(PIHP uhr ihn)* A white, crystalline substance obtained from pepper.

rock salt Common salt as it occurs in the earth in large crystals.

sea salt Salt (sodium chloride) obtained by the evaporation of seawater.

sodium *(SOH dee uhm)* A silvery-white soft metal found in Earth's crust.

sodium chloride *(SOH dee uhm KLAWR yd)* Ordinary table salt.

solar salt A coarse salt derived from solar evaporation of salt water.

table salt Ordinary salt for use at the table; sodium chloride.

umami *(oo MAH mee)* One of the basic elements of taste sensation which may be perceived as a meaty richness, such as that found in mushrooms or Parmesan cheese.

HELPFUL HINTS

When working in the kitchen with food, keep these helpful hints in mind to make sure your work goes smoothly and safely. Then enjoy the tasty treats you make!

- **Wash your hands** before you begin food preparation and after you've touched raw eggs or meat.
- Thoroughly **wash fruits and vegetables.**
- **Use oven mitts** when handling hot pots, pans, or trays.
- **Have an adult help** when working with knives and hot stoves or ovens.

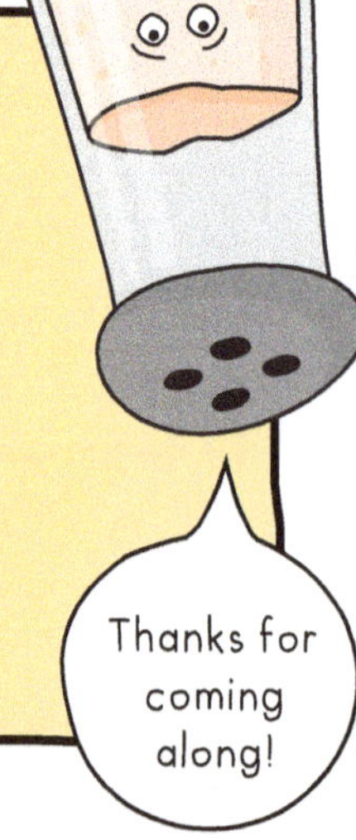

INDEX

Africa, 20-21, 40
Alexander the Great, 22, 34
allspice, 31
antipasto, 36

black pepper, 30, 32, 34, 36, 42
    recipes, 35, 37, 43
Brazil, 42
brine, 8, 16, 21, 27

Cajun seasoning, 42
carbohydrates, 37
cayenne pepper, 31
cheese salt, 24
China, 10-11, 38-39
chocolate cookies (recipe), 35
Columbus, Christopher, 40
curing, 26

da Gama, Vasco, 40

East India Company, 41
Egypt, 17, 29
Erie Canal, 26
Europe, 24-25, 34

farsan, 22
fish, 17, 24
fleur de sel, 18
France, 18

Gandhi, Mohandas K., 23
garam masala (recipe), 33
Germany, 25
glutamate, 14
Greece, ancient, 34

Himalayan salt, 19, 22, 23
hot dogs, 26-27

ice cream, 13
India, 22-23, 32-33, 40

iodized salt, 6, 24
Italy, 16, 17, 36-37

Jamaican jerk, 42
Japan, 12-13

kabobs, 21
kala namak, 23
Kerala, India, 32
khandvi, 22
Khewra Salt Mine, 19, 22
koshari, 17
kosher salt, 19
kyinkyinga, 21

lemonade, 23
lye, 16

meat, 21, 26
    recipe, 43
Mediterranean Sea, 16-17
Mesopotamia, 16
miso, 12, 15
Morocco, 20

natron, 17
Netherlands, 24, 27, 41
New World, 42

olives, 16

pasta alla carbonara, 36
pepper and peppercorns, 5, 28-45
    types of, 30-31
    See also specific types and places
pepper shakers, 44-45
pickles (recipe), 27
piperine, 31
Polo, Marco, 38
Portugal, 40-42

pretzels (recipe), 25

ranch dip (recipe), 15
red pepper, 31
roast (recipe), 43
rock salt, 9

Sahara, 20-21
salt, 4-27, 32, 45-46
    types of, 18-19
    See also specific types and places
salt mines, 9, 20
salt shakers, 44-45
sea salt, 8, 19
Shinto, 13
sodium chloride, 7, 18
solar salt, 8
soy sauce, 11
spaghetti (recipe), 37
spices, 21, 28, 31, 34, 39
stir frying, 11
sunomono, 12
Szechuan pepper, 39

table salt, 7, 18
tastes, five basic, 10, 14
Tellicherry peppercorns, 32
trade
    pepper, 29, 34, 38, 40-42
    salt, 10, 16, 20, 23, 26

umami, 12, 14, 15
United States, 26-27

white pepper, 30, 39

Zheng He, 38

World Book, Inc.
180 North LaSalle Street
Suite 900
Chicago, Illinois 60601
USA

Copyright © 2020 (print and e-book) World Book, Inc.
All rights reserved.

This volume may not be reproduced in whole or in part in any form without prior written permission from the publisher.

WORLD BOOK and the GLOBE DEVICE are registered trademarks or trademarks of World Book, Inc.

For information about other "Taste the World!" titles, as well as other World Book print and digital publications, please go to www.worldbook.com.

For information about other World Book publications, call 1-800-WORLDBK (967-5325).

For information about sales to schools and libraries, call 1-800-975-3250 (United States) or 1-800-837-5365 (Canada).

Library of Congress Cataloging-in-Publication Data

Title: Salt and pepper.
Description: Chicago, Illinois: World Book Inc., [2020] | Series: Taste the world! | Includes index. | Contents: I am salt! I am pepper! -- What is salt? -- A look at sea salt and rock salt -- China -- Japan -- The five basic tastes -- Mediterranean -- Types of salt -- Sahara -- India -- Europe -- United States -- What is pepper? -- A look at the pepper plant -- India -- Spice routes -- Italy -- China -- Age of exploration -- New world -- A perfect pair!
Identifiers: LCCN 2019037388 | ISBN 9780716628644 (hardcover) | ISBN 9780716628583 (set)
Subjects: LCSH: Salt--Juvenile literature. | Pepper (Spice)--Juvenile literature.
Classification: LCC TN900 .S25 2020 | DDC 641.3/384--dc23
LC record available at https://lccn.loc.gov/2019037388

Taste the World!
ISBN: 978-0-7166-2858-3 (set, hc.)

Salt and Pepper
ISBN: 978-0-7166-2864-4 (hc.)

Also available as:
ISBN: 978-0-7166-2872-9 (e-book)

2nd printing July 2020

STAFF

Editorial

Writer: Shawn Brennan

Manager, New Product Development
Nick Kilzer

Proofreader: Nathalie Strassheim

Manager, Contracts and Compliance
(Rights and Permissions): Loranne K. Shields

Manager, Indexing Services
David Pofelski

Digital

Director, Digital Product Development
Erika Meller

Digital Product Manager
Jonathan Wills

Graphics and Design

Coordinator, Design Development
and Production
Brenda Tropinski

Senior Visual Communications Designer
Melanie Bender

Media Editor: Rosalia Bledsoe

Senior Web Designer/Digital Media Developer
Matt Carrington

Manufacturing/Production

Manufacturing Manager: Anne Fritzinger

Production Specialist: Curley Hunter

ACKNOWLEDGMENTS

Cover   © Andrea Skjold Mink, Shutterstock; © Andrii Horulko, Shutterstock
Character artwork by Matthew Carrington
2-3   © Shutterstock; © Bauer Syndication/StockFood; © Hong Vo, iStockphoto
4-5   © Jamie Grill Photography/Getty Images; © Matyi012345/Shutterstock
6-7   © Sebastian Studio/Shutterstock; © Floriana/Getty Images
8-9   © Michel Arnault, Shutterstock; © Richard Lautens, Toronto Star/Getty Images; © Vvoe/Shutterstock; © Omihay/Shutterstock
10-11   © Bob Henry, Alamy Images; © Elena Eryomenko, Shutterstock
12-13   © Dolly MJ/Shutterstock; © FS11/Shutterstock; © Clare Lawrence, EyeEm/Getty Images
14-15   © Shutterstock
16-17   © Hong Vo, iStockphoto; © Dina Saeed, Shutterstock; © Ulrike Holsten, StockFood/age fotostock
18-19   © Edelmar/iStockphoto; © Night And Day Images/iStockphoto; © Natalya Bond, Shutterstock;

   © Michelle Lee Photography/Shutterstock; © Aimee M Lee, Shutterstock
20-21   © Gusman/Bridgeman Images; © Vasara/Shutterstock; © AS Food Studio/Shutterstock
22-23   © Shutterstock
24-25   © Frans Lemmens, Getty Images; © Plateresca/Shutterstock; © Andrea Skjold Mink, Shutterstock; © Media Photos/Getty Images
26-35   © Shutterstock
36-37   © Lauri Patterson, Getty Images; © Alexander Prokopenko, Shutterstock
38-39   © Raw F8/Shutterstock; © North Wind Picture Archives/Alamy Images; © AS Food Studio/Shutterstock
40-41   © Shutterstock
42-43   WORLD BOOK photo by Rosalia Bledsoe; © News Life Media/StockFood/age fotostock
44-45   © Sjo/Getty Images; © Andrey Nikitin, Shutterstock; © Denys Skorikov, Shutterstock; © Mark R Coons, Shutterstock; © Photos SS/Shutterstock; © Alp Aksoy, Shutterstock

www.ingramcontent.com/pod-product-compliance
Lightning Source LLC
Chambersburg PA
CBHW041048050726
47599CB00018B/2081